Managing **PTSD**

Stephanie Lundquist-Arora

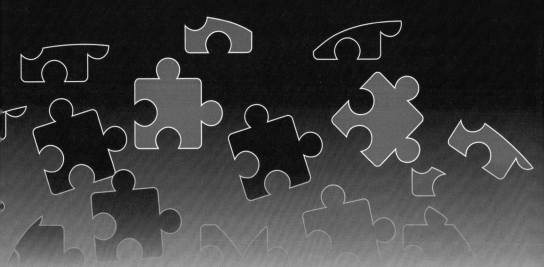

ReferencePoint Press®

San Diego, CA

About the Author

Stephanie Lundquist-Arora has master's degrees in political science and public administration. She has written several books for teens and children, including *Addiction: A Problem of Epidemic Proportions*. When not writing, Lundquist-Arora likes traveling with her family, jogging, learning jiujitsu, reading, painting, and trying new foods.

© 2022 ReferencePoint Press, Inc.
Printed in the United States

For more information, contact:
ReferencePoint Press, Inc.
PO Box 27779
San Diego, CA 92198
www.ReferencePointPress.com

LIBRARY OF CONGRESS CATALOGING-IN-PUBLICATION DATA

Names: Lundquist-Arora, Stephanie, author.
Title: Managing PTSD / by Stephanie Lundquist-Arora.
Description: San Diego, CA : ReferencePoint Press, 2022. | Series: Managing mental health | Includes bibliographical references and index.
Identifiers: LCCN 2021014898 (print) | LCCN 2021014899 (ebook) | ISBN 9781678201128 (library binding) | ISBN 9781678201135 (ebook)
Subjects: LCSH: Post-traumatic stress disorder. | Post-traumatic stress disorder--Treatment.
Classification: LCC RC552.P67 L86 2022 (print) | LCC RC552.P67 (ebook) | DDC 616.85/21--dc23
LC record available at https://lccn.loc.gov/2021014898
LC ebook record available at https://lccn.loc.gov/2021014899

Contents

The Challenges of PTSD

P.K. Philips experienced the symptoms of post-traumatic stress disorder (PTSD) for nearly two decades before she was diagnosed. Philips had suffered multiple incidents of abuse as a child. After she was raped at knifepoint in her teens, she saw the face of her attacker every time she closed her eyes. She also continues to suffer from flashbacks and nightmares. For a few years following her attack, Philips felt unsafe in her house, compulsively checking doors and windows to make sure they were locked. For decades, she believed she had a panic problem. When another traumatic event that occurred in her thirties led Philips to get help, she was diagnosed with PTSD. Relieved to discover that her symptoms were real and treatable, Philips writes, "I'm no longer at the mercy of my disorder and I would not be here today had I not had the proper diagnosis and treatment."[1]

Untreated PTSD

According to the National Institute of Mental Health, a federal agency that researches mental disorders, PTSD is caused by experiencing or witnessing a shocking or life-threatening event. There are many people like Philips who experience trauma and are subsequently afflicted with

PTSD. But not all people who go through a horrific event develop this disorder. The Sidran Institute, a nonprofit organization that provides information about and treats PTSD, finds that while 70 percent of people experience trauma in their lifetime, only up to 20 percent of those people will get PTSD.

When PTSD is not carefully managed with awareness, therapy, or medication, it can negatively impact all areas of a person's life. For example, imagine that a man who is held at gunpoint, assaulted, and robbed suffers from PTSD afterward. That person might be plagued by nightmares of robbery that interrupt his sleep, causing irritability during the day. His case

> "I'm no longer at the mercy of my disorder and I would not be here today had I not had the proper diagnosis and treatment."[1]
>
> —P.K. Philips, PTSD survivor

might be so severe that he fears leaving his home because just being outside triggers his memories of the incident. Whereas beforehand, being held at gunpoint seemed statistically improbable, he sees danger and violence around every corner and constantly fears for his life. In such a case, he would have a hard time going to school or work. He might lose his job. Maybe he no longer maintains his social relationships because he does not have an interest in taking the perceived risk of meeting others out in the world beyond the walls of his house. Because he does not care to be in public, maybe maintaining good health with exercise is no longer a priority. Drinking alcohol heavily might become a way that he avoids thinking about the trauma. In this scenario, one incident is not simply a short-term memory—like remembering what clothes were worn last Thursday. Instead, for this person, the memory of the few moments of that one trauma becomes etched in every corner of his mind and influences nearly every decision he makes.

Getting Help

Tate Mallory, a police officer from South Dakota who worked as a military-contracted police trainer in Iraq, experienced severe

After a tornado, a young man grieves amid the ruins of his house. PTSD can afflict those who experience or witness a shocking or life-threatening event such as a destructive natural disaster.

PTSD after he was gravely wounded in an attack in 2006 during the US occupation of that country. A rocket-propelled grenade hit his Humvee. The grenade entered his body via his lower back, traveled through his abdomen, and exited his inner thigh. Because it did not explode and marines rushed him to a combat hospital, he lived through the attack. When he returned home, he suffered significant psychological wounds from the trauma.

In an interview with the *New York Times*, Mallory reports that he experienced untreated symptoms of PTSD. He isolated himself and turned against his family. He was also severely depressed. About three months after the attack, he did not want to live any longer and asked his brother to kill him. Mallory's brother recalls, "What I saw was how hollow his eyes were. I'm a hunter, and to

6

me, it was like when you come up on your deer, when you didn't get a clean kill, and they just want it to be over."[2] The request prompted Mallory's brother to help him seek medical care. Under doctor's orders, Mallory began taking antidepressants and participating in counseling.

Challenges to Seeking Treatment and Managing PTSD

There are many challenges associated with seeking treatment for PTSD. Sufferers might find it difficult expressing and controlling their emotions and trusting others. They might fear how society will view them once they are diagnosed. Those with PTSD might also fail to seek help because they isolate themselves or face other disorders like depression and substance abuse that stem from their trauma.

Even when diagnosed, PTSD can be difficult to manage. Trauma is often stored as a long-term memory throughout the brain. Any taste, smell, sight, sound, or texture is capable of bringing the nightmarish experience to the surface for those who suffer from PTSD. Despite its challenges, PTSD can be managed, and those individuals do regain control of their lives with the right assistance. Philips writes, "There are things I can do to ensure that I never have to suffer as I did before being diagnosed with PTSD. . . . The most important thing to know is that it's never too late to seek help."[3]

Chapter One

When the Brain Gets Stuck in Danger Mode

Eva Holland experienced symptoms of PTSD following several car accidents. In the worst of Holland's accidents, a U-Haul truck coming from the opposite direction crossed the yellow line into her lane. She narrowly avoided a head-on collision by swerving onto the shoulder of her lane. The truck sideswiped her vehicle, breaking her windshield and covering her with shards of glass. Following the accident and before treatment, Holland felt panicked and often experienced flashbacks whenever she had to drive. In the *New York Times*, she writes, "I felt certain that I would crash again, and that this time I would die. Sometimes on the highway I had to pull over to hyperventilate and sob."[4]

For people not in the military, car accidents are the leading cause of PTSD. According to Resources to Recover, which shares free online services for positive mental health outcomes, 25 to 33 percent of car accident survivors develop PTSD. They tend to have avoidance behaviors, in which they abstain from driving, refuse to get in a car, or stay off certain roads. PTSD UK, a charity that raises awareness about PTSD, states that such avoidance behaviors might increase the trauma survivors' likelihood of developing the disorder because it strengthens their existing belief that driving is always dangerous. Moreover, the survivors' fear response to driving remains high. In other words, someone with PTSD physiologically responds to a harmless act like getting into a car as though it were dangerous.

> "I felt certain that I would crash again, and that this time I would die. Sometimes on the highway I had to pull over to hyperventilate and sob."[4]
>
> —Eva Holland, car crash survivor

Symptoms of PTSD

Traumatic events naturally trigger the fight-or-flight response for those involved. The fight-or-flight response, also called hyper-arousal, occurs when the perceived threat stimulates the nervous system (specifically, the amygdala part of the brain) to initiate the body's physiological response to stress. A person in this state experiences an adrenaline boost—leading to a quicker heart rate,

Firefighters extricate victims of a car crash. Car accidents are the leading cause of PTSD.

racing thoughts, and tense muscles. The response offers natural superpowers to either flee or resist a situation in order to increase a person's chances of survival. When the threat is gone, another part of the brain (the prefrontal cortex) sends a signal to return the body to its regular state. In some cases, a traumatic incident causes the amygdala to remain active while the prefrontal cortex takes a break. In brief, with PTSD the brain gets paused while it is operating in danger mode.

In some cases people who experience trauma begin to have symptoms associated with PTSD within one month of an incident. Other times the reaction is delayed further. In cases of delayed-onset PTSD, the first episode of the disorder might occur six or more months after the traumatic event. The symptoms of PTSD, whether delayed onset or immediate, are vast and vary case by case. According to the Mayo Clinic, a nonprofit American medical center, PTSD symptoms cluster around three main categories of the brain's response: reliving the trauma, avoidance, and hypervigilance.

Reliving the Trauma

When people experience a traumatic event, sometimes their brain fixates on the dangerous moment in time as a way of processing it. Those diagnosed with PTSD suffer from intrusive memories of the trauma, which include flashbacks, recurrent memories, and nightmares. In the case of flashbacks, the afflicted persons usually experience stimuli that put them back into the moment when they first felt the threat of danger.

The Fourth of July is a difficult day for American military veterans who suffer from PTSD. The noise from the fireworks sometimes simulates experiences of gunfire and mortar attacks while they were in combat. Army veteran Henry Ximenez, who suffers from PTSD, experiences flashbacks when he hears fireworks. Ximenez tells Washington, DC, news network WUSA9 that while other people are outside celebrating Independence Day, his reaction to fireworks is to "squat and drop down and just put my hands over my head."[5]

A high percentage of people who are diagnosed with PTSD experience recurrent nightmares. These individuals relive the original traumatic event through dreams, flashbacks, and repeating memories.

Others who are diagnosed with PTSD further experience trauma in recurrent nightmares. The National Center for PTSD, a research and education center on PTSD, finds that of the people who are diagnosed with the disorder, 71 to 96 percent of them have nightmares. Some PTSD survivors report having multiple nightmares each week, according to the organization. Healthline, a health information website, reports that nightmares can have many negative effects on those who suffer from PTSD, including worsening symptoms, reducing sleep quality, and contributing to the onset of depression. Nightmares, flashbacks, and recurrent memories are ways the brain of a person afflicted with PTSD re-lives the original traumatic event.

Avoidance

After the traumatic event, PTSD sufferers also avoid certain thoughts or feelings, activities, people, or places that were once part of their regular lives. The National Center for PTSD explains that avoiding thoughts or feelings is called emotional avoidance.

On May 22, 2017, a terrorist bomb killed twenty-two people and injured hundreds more at an Ariana Grande concert in Manchester, England. Many were left to cope with the mental injuries of experiencing such trauma either first- or secondhand.

An article in the journal *Current Opinion in Psychiatry* finds that 28 to 35 percent of people exposed to a terrorist attack develop PTSD. Ruth Murrell is among them. Murrell and her daughter, who was twelve years old at the time, were both physically injured during the bombing at the Grande concert. In an interview with the *Independent*, Murrell says, "The physical injuries were serious but the mental side was very much harder to deal with. I couldn't cope. There was a period when I couldn't sleep, couldn't eat and was vomiting constantly." Survivors Against Terror, a support group for terrorism survivors, suggests that these symptoms are common. The group's surveys find that terrorism victims often suffer in silence and that some do not reach out for support for PTSD symptoms until more than a year after the trauma.

Quoted in Alex Matthews-King, "Mental Health Crisis Failing UK Victims of Terror Attacks, Report Warns," *The Independent* (London), November 20, 2018. www.independent.co.uk.

In the case of emotional avoidance, people with PTSD attempt to shut down memories associated with the trauma they have experienced. Combat veterans might try not to think about their deployment to avoid memories of the times their lives were in grave danger. Some sufferers use alcohol or drugs to keep those memories at bay. When people with PTSD are using emotional avoidance, which occurs internally in their minds, it is often more difficult for their loved ones to notice than when they are engaging in behavioral avoidance.

When PTSD survivors use behavioral avoidance, they purposely stop seeing people, going to places, or engaging in activities that remind them of their trauma. Rape survivors with PTSD, for example, report trying to avoid going out in public. HeretoHelp, a nonprofit agency that provides information on mental health and substance use, reports that Sharon was twenty-one years old when a male date raped her. She had met the man in one of her classes while studying at a university. After the trauma, she stopped going to her university for fear of seeing her attacker. She also withdrew from her family members. Well after the trauma, Sharon still reports doubts that she would experience intimacy with a man again. She also avoids watching movies with rape scenes and tries not to go out in public.

Sharon's behavioral avoidance is typical for rape survivors, but psychologists argue it is not productive for their mental health. Victims of rape and other PTSD survivors find that therapy helps them confront their trauma and put an end to emotional and behavioral avoidance. Shaili Jain, a psychiatrist, emphasizes the importance of overcoming avoidance when she writes, "Avoiding trauma only allows PTSD to thrive. Fully confronting avoidance in ourselves, our loved ones and society means finally overcoming the biggest obstacle to our becoming a truly trauma-informed society."[6]

> "Avoiding trauma only allows PTSD to thrive. Fully confronting avoidance in ourselves, our loved ones and society means finally overcoming the biggest obstacle to our becoming a truly trauma-informed society."[6]
>
> —Shaili Jain, psychiatrist

Hypervigilance

In addition to avoidance and reliving trauma, PTSD survivors also experience the symptom of hypervigilance. Hypervigilance is a heightened state of alertness in which a person is tense and has an exaggerated fear of danger. People who are chronically hypervigilant are trying to protect themselves by always searching for the danger around them. Matthew Tull, a professor of psychology at the University of Toledo, explains that hypervigilance in those with PTSD is an obstacle to a higher quality of life because it "can leave [them] exhausted while interfering with interpersonal relationships, work, and [their] ability to function on a day-to-day basis."[7]

Hypervigilance causes a change in the afflicted person's reaction to stimuli. Because of the increased amount of adrenaline, a person with PTSD might have an increased startle reflex. For many combat veterans, a balloon popping brings to mind the sound of a weapon that went off just before their friends died and they almost lost their own life. A freelance writer who goes by the user name eristarisis describes a combat veteran friend (using the pronoun *they* to protect gender identity) who had an adverse reaction to a balloon popping at a party. Eristarisis writes, "Acting on pure reflex and terror, they executed a full combat dive and roll to cover the nearest pillar—and I saw their right hand scrambling to draw a nonexistent sidearm from a nonexistent holster."[8] These types of hypervigilant reactions to balloons popping are not atypical in combat veterans.

Traumatic Events That Cause PTSD

According to the National Center for PTSD, 7 to 8 percent of the US population will experience PTSD at some point in their life. The most common causes of PTSD are combat, sexual or physical abuse, natural disasters, and car accidents. While constituting a smaller percentage of total PTSD cases, other causes include but are not limited to childbirth, sudden death of a loved one, witnessing a mass shooting or terrorist attack, and working as a first responder. These events might bring about symptoms immediately or over time, and the pain of living with PTSD can linger and resurface throughout a person's life.

Delayed Reactions

PTSD symptoms are not always apparent immediately following a traumatic event, and they might worsen with time if untreated. The National Center for PTSD finds that people who experience trauma and lack social support or have continued hardships are more likely to experience PTSD symptoms. Lisa Williams, a psychologist and chief executive officer of a nonprofit providing mental health services to tornado victims, explains that research examining Hurricane Katrina victims shows that mental health needs actually increase five to seven years after a natural disaster.

In 2018, four years after a deadly tornado devastated Moore, Oklahoma, fourteen-year-old Xavier Delgado, who was likely afflicted with PTSD, committed suicide. Delgado was ten years old when the destructive tornado tore into his elementary school with its 210-mile-per-hour (338 kph) winds and took twenty-four lives in its path. Forty minutes after the tornado had passed, first responders found Delgado under a pile of rubble with a piece of debris piercing his abdomen. At first, he appeared to be emotionally unaffected. He was even joking around with the nurses in the hospital. When he was released from the hospital and watching coverage of the storm on television, he counted the number of friends who died in the tornado on seven of his fingers. His seven-year-old sister was nearly one of them. She was in a different classroom when flying debris knocked her unconscious, and the tornado carried her 10 yards (9.1 m) away.

Shortly after the tornado, it became clearer that Delgado was more affected than it first appeared. Delgado's mother said that her son stopped doing the things he enjoyed, like in-line skating and flying on airplanes, because he was consumed by the fear of death. His pediatrician attributed some of his behavioral changes to attention-deficit/hyperactivity disorder. She further told Delgado's mother that children are resilient and that her son would bounce back. A different doctor later said that Delgado likely had PTSD and survivor's guilt, which is when a survivor feels guilt for living through a traumatic event during which others have perished. After he took his life, Delgado's friend, Lola Ochoa, said that she had not known he was struggling. In a local news interview, she stated, "He didn't want to show that he was hurting because he just wanted to be that fun person."[9]

Lingering Impact of PTSD

Victims of physical abuse also experience lasting PTSD symptoms. Twenty-five-year-old Sophia (a false name to protect her identity) was diagnosed with PTSD following an abusive relationship with her former boyfriend. He broke her rib, left multiple bruises on her body, choked her until she went unconscious, and called her derogatory names. He also raped her. During an episode of abuse, Sophia managed to escape and ran to her friend's house. She pressed charges, and her abuser spent time in jail.

Long after Sophia's bruises healed, she continued to experience mental consequences of the abuse. Immediately after Sophia ended the relationship, a friend helped care for her. Sophia was afraid to be alone. Any noise in her apartment terrified her. Any slight disturbance caused her heart rate to increase, her body to shake, and a stress rash to spread across her face and neck. She also feared leaving the apartment because she was scared that her abuser would find her. About six months after she escaped from him, she was officially diagnosed with PTSD. Even with treatment, the memories of abuse plague Sophia's mind. She explains that, as she was raped on a winter night, the weather triggers her symptoms. In an interview with the online magazine *Self*, she says, "That winter was the snowiest I can remember, and watching snow fall brings it all rushing back."[10]

Like Sophia, many people are victims of domestic violence at some point in their lives. In the United States an average of twenty-four people per minute are the victim of rape, physical abuse, or stalking by an intimate partner—totaling 12 million men and women each year, according to the Centers for Disease Control and Prevention's National Intimate Partner and Sexual Violence Survey published in 2017. PTSD following physical abuse and rape is common. Recovery Village, which provides information and offers treatment services for substance abuse and co-occurring mental health disorders, reports that 49 percent of rape victims and 32 percent of severe physical assault victims experience PTSD. In the case of domestic violence, Recovery Village further suggests that the strong bond between the victim and the abuser likely plays a significant role in making the abuse that much more traumatic.

> "That winter was the snowiest I can remember, and watching snow fall brings it all rushing back."[10]
>
> —Sophia, rape survivor

The Sudden Death of a Family Member and the Stress of Carrying On

Though not as common, the sudden death of a loved one is also a trauma that can cause PTSD. Erin Donovan suffered from the mental health disorder after her mother died from injuries sustained during a car accident. Donovan's mother was driving down a country road in heavy rain when the tires began to slide onto the gravel on the side. When she overcorrected, she crossed the yellow line and ran into the side of an oncoming truck that was pulling a trailer. Because of the accident, Donovan's mother had a partially collapsed lung, brain injuries, and paralysis on the right side of her body. For nearly three weeks after the accident,

The sudden death of a loved one can be both traumatic and a cause of PTSD. Although physical trauma is more commonly associated with PTSD, mental and emotional trauma can also trigger this condition.

breathing and feeding tubes kept her alive, but she never regained brain function. Donovan had to make the decision to remove her mother from life support. Without life support, her mother died three days later.

Donovan spent the following months cleaning out her mother's house and dealing with a lawsuit against her mother's estate connected to the accident, until she could not handle it anymore. She felt overwhelmed and longed to ask her mother for advice. She writes, "I had to remind myself, repeatedly, that my mom was dead. If I can imagine what it feels like to have dementia, this might be it. Having to be told the same bad news again and again and again."[11] Donovan also obsessively imagined the violence her mother experienced in the accident. She went to a therapist, who diagnosed her with PTSD.

The diagnosis surprised Donovan because she had not experienced any physical trauma. Regarding having PTSD, Donovan writes, "What? Isn't that for like, combat veterans and war refugees? Rape survivors or people who escape cults? I mean, nothing happened *to* me."[12] She acknowledges that at the time, she did not understand that PTSD results not only from physical trauma but mental trauma as well. In a study published in 2016 in the medical journal *Depression and Anxiety*, an average of 5.2 percent of respondents experienced PTSD following the death of a loved one. The same study found that women were three times more likely than men to experience PTSD following the death of a loved one.

Managing Trauma over Time

When someone experiences trauma, the effects can last long past the event itself. The psychological consequences might extend beyond the injuries to the body that were sustained during the trauma. PTSD symptoms, though manageable, sometimes last a lifetime. An article in the academic journal *Psychotherapy: Theory, Research, Practice, Training* explains why trauma affects the brain so extensively. The authors write, "Because during trauma it is usually not safe or possible for individuals to consciously access their emotional reactions or experiences, awareness often emerges after trauma ceases."[13] Only with help can individuals deal with those emotions and move on with their lives, even if the trauma never completely disappears.

Chapter Two

Scabs, Scars, and Reoccurring Injuries

Jared (a false name to protect his identity) was diagnosed with PTSD years after a combat deployment. He was raised on a farm in the Midwest and joined the US Army when he was twenty years old. A few weeks into his deployment in Afghanistan, a fellow soldier was killed in combat. That was a turning event for Jared's personality. His experience with PTSD appears on the website of the American Psychiatric Association. The account describes how he was transformed from a "happy-go-lucky farm boy to a frightened, overprotective soldier."[14] One time in Afghanistan, Jared accidentally fell asleep while on guard duty. He was startled awake by the noise of an enemy mortar.

His experiences during combat stayed with him after his return home. In the years that followed, he earned an undergraduate degree as well as a graduate degree in business, and he got married and had children. Even though life marched on, Jared suffered intrusive memories, nightmares, and flashbacks from his time in combat. He was also hypervigilant, always on alert for potential danger. The symptoms he was most concerned about were the anger and aggression with which he responded when startled. During a doctor's appointment, Jared dozed off on the examination table. When a nurse brushed his foot as she passed him, he jumped off the table, spewed expletives, and threatened her. The response frightened both him and the nurse. Jared knew he needed help. At age thirty-six, sixteen years following his army enlistment, he was diagnosed with PTSD at the US Department of Veterans Affairs (VA) outpatient mental health clinic.

PTSD and Veterans

Many veterans, like Jared, are diagnosed with PTSD following combat deployments. According to the National Center for PTSD, 11 to 20 percent of veterans of military missions in Operation Iraqi Freedom (2003–2011) and Operation Enduring Freedom (2001–2014) have PTSD in a given year. Meanwhile, the American Psychological Association reports that an estimated 30 percent of veterans of the Vietnam War have experienced PTSD. That is significantly higher than the estimated 3 percent of the US population (with the veterans included) experiencing PTSD in a given year. But PTSD is not unique to US military members. The *European Journal of Psychotraumatology* reported in 2019 that about 354 million survivors of war globally suffer from PTSD, serious depression, or both. In other words, people who have been around combat are much more likely than those who have not to experience PTSD.

US Army veteran Isiah James, who deployed twice to Iraq and once to Afghanistan, is among those experiencing PTSD. James, who was an infantryman, says he loved being in the military and enjoyed its camaraderie before being forcibly retired when he was twenty-seven due to an injury. Following his third deployment and subsequent retirement, he considered suicide. That is when he realized he needed help. In an interview with Boston radio station WBUR, he says, "I was sitting in my bathroom on the floor with a giant bottle of scotch and a bottle of sleeping pills and just crying uncontrollably . . . not wanting to live with this anymore because

Long deployments and the terrifying experiences that come with being in a war zone lead to higher rates of PTSD among military personnel than is found in the civilian population.

I have seen so much pain and so much death and destruction throughout my deployments."[15] The following day, James went to a VA clinic to seek help.

Delayed-Onset PTSD

Like with James, sometimes the reaction to trauma is delayed for various reasons. For him, social isolation after he retired from the military contributed to his PTSD. He says, "I didn't really deal with [PTSD] while I was in [the army] because . . . everybody is going through the same things. But it's when you get outside the military . . . and you're on your own and you don't really have that support network there."[16]

Delayed-onset PTSD happens when the first episode of PTSD occurs six or more months after the traumatic event. The first PTSD symptoms from the trauma might occur even more than a year after the event. People experience trauma in different ways. The lack of a formal PTSD diagnosis is not necessarily because a person is not experiencing any symptoms. Following a trauma, people might have nightmares, for example, but not enough to suggest that they have PTSD. Symptoms from the original trauma sometimes worsen when a person subsequently experiences increased anxiety.

When a person has experienced trauma, future events can trigger latent PTSD symptoms. Kenneth Vail, an assistant professor of psychology at Cleveland State University, uses a levee simile to explain why trauma in later years intensifies PTSD symptoms from earlier events. Vail suggests that the psychological system people have in place to shut out anxieties and fears of death is like a levee. A levee is a large barrier that prevents a river from overflowing and destroying everything in its path. According to Vail's comparison, the psychological levee is made up of an individual's value system and self-esteem. Because prior trauma affects a person's value system and self-esteem, the individual is likely more susceptible to the PTSD symptoms associated with a second trauma later on. In short, the second event is like a psychological storm straining and eventually rupturing the levee banks. Vail writes, "When the psychological storm hits and the levee breaks, in washes a flood of death-related thoughts and anxieties."[17]

"I didn't really deal with [PTSD] while I was in [the army] because . . . everybody is going through the same things. But it's when you get outside the military . . . and you're on your own and you don't really have that support network there."[16]

—Isiah James, combat veteran

Retired police officer John Driscoll's metaphorical levee broke during one such psychological storm. Driscoll, who experienced a physical attack when he was seven years old, had PTSD but was not diagnosed until many years later. Following the initial trauma, he had insomnia and spent hours in his classrooms thinking about how he could prevent attacks like the one he experienced. In adulthood, Driscoll's PTSD affected his professional and personal life long before he was diagnosed.

As a police officer, Driscoll explains that his breaking point was when a young girl was murdered next to his police station. After Driscoll responded to the scene, a coworker found him crying on the floor of the police station and took him home. That was the last time he ever wore his uniform. Being upset about a young girl's murder is a common reaction for anyone, but Driscoll explains that the images permeated all aspects of his life. He writes, "The young girl's death did more than linger in my mind. Once again, the intrusive images pierced my every thought. Only now the thoughts were more frequent and represented all the negative events from throughout my life."[18] Driscoll sought professional help to manage his PTSD. While he still has difficult days, he is thankful for treatment and says that without it he might have lost his family. The avoidance, flashbacks, and stress associated with the mental health disorder are widely known to impact the afflicted person's professional life and interpersonal relationships.

People experience trauma in different ways. Some experience immediate effects while others tamp down their anxieties and fears until they burst forth.

Driscoll says he did not seek help earlier in his life because he was worried about the stigma attached to PTSD. He did not want to lose his job or have his coworkers to see him as weak. The stigmatization of the PTSD diagnosis is a hurdle that can prevent some people from seeking help. But Driscoll believes that if he had gotten treatment earlier he might have been able to avoid reaching his breaking point. His case highlights the importance of seeking treatment and managing the early symptoms of PTSD.

> "The young girl's death did more than linger in my mind. . . . Only now the thoughts were more frequent and represented all the negative events from throughout my life."[18]
>
> —John Driscoll, former police officer

Acute Stress Disorder

Early symptoms of trauma might not evolve into PTSD but might reflect the more temporary acute stress disorder (ASD). Immediately following the traumatic event, it is not uncommon to experience ASD, in which symptoms such as nightmares and a more sensitive startle reflex persist for weeks, rather than months or years. In many cases following traffic accidents, for example, those involved have intrusive memories of the event, try to avoid driving, and have an increased sense of paranoia regarding the danger of being in vehicles. Sometimes, the symptoms go away within a few weeks. In those cases, people likely experienced ASD, not PTSD, following their traumas.

According to the National Center for PTSD, of people who witness or experience a traumatic event, 6 to 33 percent suffer from ASD, depending on the type of event. Survivors of violent crimes such as robbery, for example, have higher rates of ASD than those who experience natural disasters. A 2009 journal article published in *Psychiatric Clinics of North America* finds that 80 percent of people with ASD develop PTSD. If the symptoms last for more than a month, the condition is more likely to be PTSD. In brief, ASD is like a brain scab, whereas PTSD is more like a scar. In a 2018 article for Healthline, psychologist and nurse practitioner Timothy Legg and nurse Rose Kivi suggest that seeking medical treatment within a few hours of the trauma may help reduce the risk of developing ASD and PTSD.

Relapsing Symptoms

People who experience PTSD sometimes find that their symptoms come and go. With treatment, they might find that they are without symptoms for a length of time. A relapse occurs when a person who has undergone treatment and as a result has stopped experiencing the symptoms begins having them again. The early warning signs of PTSD relapse, according to Verywell Mind, an online mental health resource, include changes in mood, behavior, and thought. PTSD relapse is often brought on by increased stress, isolation, or another traumatic event.

PTSD survivors further are vulnerable to relapse because of images in the media. Consultant360, a media platform with case briefings for practitioners intended to improve patient care, details the case of Ms. N, a sixty-four-year-old who went to her physician because she had headaches and difficulty sleeping. When the doctor asked when her headaches first began, Ms. N became emotional and cried. Her symptoms occurred when she started watching the coverage of the 2004 earthquake and tsunami in the Indian Ocean. She told her doctor that she could not stop thinking about the images she had seen on the news of dead children strewn along the shores of South Asia. She even pictured herself among them.

Ms. N told her doctor that as a young child, her parents had sexually, physically, and emotionally abused her. When she was eight years old, her parents were sentenced to prison for beating and killing her two younger brothers. Her life in foster care afterward was also traumatic. Six years later, at age fourteen, Ms. N was educated in a religious boarding school, where she eventually attained her high school diploma. Since completing a secretarial program, Ms. N has worked for a law firm for thirty-five years and

Teen Experiences PTSD After Witnessing Mass Shooting

Like adults, young people can also suffer symptoms of PTSD after a trauma. One of the frequently cited traumas that causes PTSD in children and teens is being witnesses or victims of violent crimes or mass shootings.

Emely Vazquez is among the survivors of the mass shooting at Marjory Stoneman Douglas High School in Parkland, Florida. On February 14, 2018, a former student opened fire in the school with a semiautomatic rifle, killing seventeen people and wounding seventeen others. Vazquez sat quietly in the corner of a darkened classroom with her classmates and teacher as the assailant stalked the hallways. While police escorted her and other students out of the school immediately following the shooting, she saw the body bags covering the victims in the hallway.

Vasquez is one of many teens from the Parkland shooting who suffer from PTSD. Even with therapy and medication, she is triggered by sounds and events that remind her of the shooting. She further suffers from depression, anxiety, and survivor's guilt. In an interview with CBS News, she says, "You almost feel guilty that they were the ones who died. Like you should have taken it for them instead." Her mother fears that the symptoms will stay with Emely for the rest of her life.

Quoted in CBS News, "Parkland School Shooting Survivors Say They're Suffering from PTSD," June 19, 2019. www.cbsnews.com.

chooses to live a single, solitary life. She works long hours and reports feeling safer at her desk at the law firm than in her home. Ms. N, who was suffering a PTSD relapse, told her doctor that the media coverage of people finding their dead family members was disturbing and that she could not escape from the images.

Isolation and media coverage during the COVID-19 pandemic have also contributed to relapse for PTSD survivors. Sergio Alfaro, an army combat medic veteran, was diagnosed with PTSD after his return from the war in Iraq. He describes being afraid to walk down the streets of Chicago when he returned from combat because he thought someone might try to hurt him. In an interview with the American Homefront Project, which reports on American military life and veterans, he explains that some of the gains he made in dealing with his symptoms have been challenged by the pandemic. He says, "Now I have that sense of danger creeping back into my life again. Is that something I'm going to catch? Am I also going to be putting my family's lives at risk as well?"[19] Alfaro explains that avoiding people, however, actually fuels his depression and worsens his PTSD symptoms.

Factors Influencing the Likelihood of Developing PTSD

Isolation influences the likelihood of developing PTSD following a traumatic situation. Each year, about 8 million adults in America have PTSD, which is only a small percentage of the total number of people who have experienced trauma. A complex system of brain development, experience, and demographics affects the likelihood that someone who experiences a terrifying event will subsequently develop PTSD. Personality traits, genetics, age during trauma, mental health history, exposure to prior trauma, and

Police officers and others who work in high-stress jobs are more likely to experience anxiety than people who work in other types of jobs. Unchecked anxiety combined with other factors increases vulnerability to post-traumatic stress.

the extent to which one was involved in the trauma (experiencing or witnessing) all affect one's likelihood of developing PTSD.

The type of trauma also influences whether and to what extent someone will suffer from PTSD. A study published in *Psychology Today* in 2020 found that respondents in the high-symptom category were more likely to report experiencing combat or sexual abuse. They were also more likely to be younger when they first developed symptoms and to have experienced PTSD for longer than people in other groups. Finally, a higher percentage of women than men in the study reported experiencing intense symptoms.

Aside from the type of trauma one suffers, gender also influences a person's likelihood of developing PTSD after a horrific event. According to the National Center for PTSD, about 10 percent of women develop PTSD sometime in their life, compared with about 4 percent of men. A 2017 article published by the *European Journal of Psychotraumatology* found that women are more likely to experience PTSD than men because they are more likely to experience sexual assault and because there are gender differences in the brain affecting responses to trauma. The National Center for PTSD also finds that women are more likely to develop PTSD because they are more likely than men to blame themselves for the trauma.

In a 2020 study, experts from the New York University (NYU) School of Medicine found that a combination of genetic and emotional differences led to post-traumatic stress (PTS), the mental anxiety common to people who work in a high-stress job in which experiencing trauma is more likely. Investigators collected data from 207 police officers afflicted with PTS in New York City, San Francisco, Oakland, and San Jose who had experienced at least one life-threatening trauma during their first year with the police force. Police officers are particularly vulnerable to developing PTS, and subsequently PTSD, because they experience an average of three traumas every six months on the job. The study concludes that the most significant indicators for one's likelihood of developing PTS include a sensitive startle reflex, preexisting symptoms of anxiety and depression, and genetic differences (such as mutation in the HDC gene, which is responsible for the immune system). The findings represent a breakthrough in understanding causal factors in the development of PTSD. Charles Marmar, the study's senior author and a professor of psychiatry at the NYU School of Medicine, writes, "If we can identify major risk factors that cause PTS and treat them before they have the chance to develop into full-blown post-traumatic stress disorder, or PTSD, we can improve the quality of life for police officers and perhaps other emergency responders."[20]

The Importance of Quickly Identifying and Managing PTSD

Identifying risk factors for developing PTSD is important. Trauma affects people in different ways, and knowing risk factors

Complex PTSD

Complex post-traumatic stress disorder (C-PTSD) can develop when trauma recurs over a period of months or even years. Though it appears among prisoners of war and torture victims, it is most common in victims of domestic abuse, especially children. While the symptoms of PTSD and C-PTSD are similar, the main difference, aside from the repetitive trauma, is that C-PTSD has more intense symptoms. Individuals with C-PTSD often have difficulty regulating or even understanding their emotions. Many children with C-PTSD never encountered a loving environment before they experienced trauma, so they lack a sense of normal behavior and relationships. In some cases victims of prolonged physical abuse believe that they are to blame and long for their abuser to love them.

Beauty After Bruises, an organization focusing on outreach and awareness for victims of complex trauma, reports that even in therapy, C-PTSD survivors have a worldview that is often pessimistic, and they hold deep feelings of hopelessness and despair. Beauty After Bruises believes that there is reason to hope treatment for people with C-PTSD will be helpful. "We want to be here to help bring pause to those deep swings into the darkness—doing what we can to keep survivors in the light a little longer."

Beauty After Bruises, "What Is C-PTSD?," www.beautyafterbruises.org.

might help alleviate the PTSD burden. Sometimes symptoms do not appear for more than a year, or perhaps not at all. Other times people experience intense symptoms immediately following a trauma, but only for a few weeks. Others have a few symptoms but not enough for a diagnosis, and then they are overwhelmed with PTSD symptoms after a subsequent trauma. Some PTSD survivors experience the horrors of their trauma intermittently throughout their entire lives. Whether a scrape, a scab, a scar, or a recurring injury, experts agree that symptoms of PTSD are manageable with professional help.

"If we can identify major risk factors that cause PTS and treat them before they have the chance to develop into full-blown post-traumatic stress disorder . . . we can improve the quality of life for police officers and perhaps other emergency responders."[20]

—Charles Marmar, New York University professor of psychiatry

Chapter Three

Treatment Options

Concepción de León experienced symptoms of PTSD after she was molested multiple times as a young child. At first, she trivialized her trauma and tried to be thankful that it was not worse, but therapy made her understand the significant toll it had taken on her. In the *New York Times*, she writes, "The more I discussed my childhood experiences with Amy [Bernstein, a therapist], the more I realized that being inappropriately touched—between the ages of 6 and 9—had ruined me."[21] She reports that even though she minimized her trauma in her mind, she felt unsafe in her body as a child, and generally uncomfortable as an adult—especially during intimate moments.

De León started therapy in hopes of rewriting her trauma script to understand its magnitude and to make herself feel safe. She explains that she discounted what happened to her because she had loved the men who abused her. After discussing the trauma, one of the exercises Bernstein recommended is the soothing of the younger self. Whenever De León feels symptoms from the memories of her abuse, she pictures herself as a child with her hair in pigtails. She writes, "Sometimes, I lay in bed and voice a belated consolation for her: 'You're safe. I'm here for you now.'"[22]

Treatment Goals and Methods

Bernstein's soothing technique for De León is a common thera-peutic method used to cope with childhood trauma. Treatment programs for PTSD, which generally include a combination of psychotherapy and medication, have three goals: to alleviate symptoms, to teach the afflicted person how to live with exist-ing symptoms, and to improve self-esteem. Soothing the inner child is a method that can help with each of those goals.

Bessel van der Kolk, a profes-sor of psychiatry at Boston Univer-sity School of Medicine, explains in his book *The Body Keeps the Score: Brain, Mind, and Body in the Healing of Trauma* that there are two important approaches for recovery after trauma. The first is a top-down approach in which the traumatized person talks with others. He or she connects with friends and family, and of-ten a licensed therapist, to process his or her understanding of the trauma. The top-down approach further might include taking medication that helps alleviate hypervigilance and other related symptoms. Meanwhile, the bottom-up approach encourages the person to have new experiences that challenge the negative feel-ings (like helplessness and anger) that resulted from the trauma. Van der Kolk writes, "Which one of these is best for any particular survivor is an empirical question. Most people I have worked with require a combination."[23] Many mental health experts recommend trauma-focused psychotherapy in particular for PTSD survivors.

> "The more I discussed my childhood experiences with Amy [Bernstein, a therapist], the more I realized that being inappropriately touched—between the ages of 6 and 9—had ruined me."[21]
>
> —Concepción de León, abuse survivor

Addressing PTSD Through Psychotherapy

In fact, according to the National Center for PTSD, trauma-focused psychotherapy, which involves anywhere from eight to sixteen sessions with a licensed therapist, is the most common treatment for PTSD. In it, the patient focuses on the memory of the initial trauma and its lasting meaning. Some methods focus more on the event itself, and others on the meaning it has to the patient. A 2020 study published in *Biological Psychiatry* suggests that trauma-focused psychotherapy is successful in treating PTSD because it changes the communication networks in the brain. Untreated PTSD survivors have higher levels of communication between the emotion-centered and the logic-centered regions of the brain. Functional magnetic resonance imaging (fMRI) scans showed that after trauma-focused psychotherapy, the communication between the two regions of the brain in PTSD survivors had been reduced. This reduction in the communication leads to a lessening of PTSD symptoms in trauma survivors.

Trauma-focused therapy includes cognitive behavioral therapy, eye movement desensitization and reprocessing, and exposure-based psychotherapy. While the three types of therapy are focused on the patient's trauma, there are some key differences.

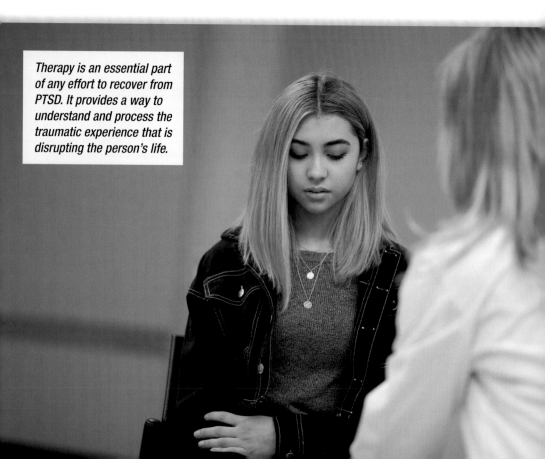

Therapy is an essential part of any effort to recover from PTSD. It provides a way to understand and process the traumatic experience that is disrupting the person's life.

Cognitive Behavioral Therapy

Cognitive behavioral therapy (CBT) focuses on helping the PTSD survivor (and others prone to panic attacks, anger issues, addiction, or other mental health conditions) identify and change negative thought patterns. One of the negative thought patterns in people with PTSD is forecasting, or predicting an event—often catastrophic—that has not happened. For example, someone who has been in a car accident might experience anxiety and forecast his or her own death or injury every time he or she rides in a car.

In CBT the first step is to identify the negative thought patterns. The next step is to practice new skills during times when the catastrophic thinking is triggered. This might include a calming meditation exercise in the backseat of a car. Another component of CBT is goal setting. With the help of a therapist, a PTSD survivor sets both short- and long-term goals for recovery. Self-monitoring progress toward the set goals gradually helps the PTSD survivor overcome destructive thought patterns. Important techniques in CBT include journaling, role playing, meditation, and mental distractions.

CBT, while helpful for some, is not the best treatment for everyone with PTSD. A 2018 study published in the journal *Biological Psychiatry: Cognitive Neuroscience and Neuroimaging* found that CBT helped improve cognitive function in people with PTSD. Critics of the approach, however, suggest that simply becoming aware of negative thought patterns does not make changing them easy. CBT patients must be willing to do a lot of homework and self-analysis on their own. Finally, this type of psychotherapy is structured, and not everyone is responsive to highly structured therapy because it tends to ignore some people's unconscious resistance to change.

Eye Movement Desensitization and Reprocessing

While CBT focuses more on the meaning of the trauma to the PTSD survivor, eye movement desensitization and reprocessing

(EMDR) therapy focuses on deflecting the pain of the trauma itself. In EMDR therapy sessions, the therapist acts as a guide for PTSD survivors while they relive their traumas in increments, during which time the therapist directs their eye movements. The therapist often has a device that beeps to help regulate the patients' eye movements from side to side under their eyelids. Mental health experts who support EMDR for trauma therapy believe that remembering stressful events is less traumatic when people are distracted by regulating their eye movements. Over time, EMDR is intended to lessen the emotional impact of the trauma on the patient.

Eva Holland suffered from PTSD symptoms following a series of car accidents. She had feelings of panic, suffered flashbacks, and experienced catastrophic thinking while driving. Holland engaged in EMDR therapy to alleviate these symptoms. Her therapist asked questions as she relived the car accidents while moving her eyes. In later sessions, the therapist used a technique called resource installation, in which Holland was told to think of a memory that made her feel safe. As her eyes shifted back and forth, Holland thought about her loving grandmother. To her surprise, the memory during EMDR made her feel stronger. The therapy worked for Holland. In the New York Times, she writes, "E.M.D.R. taught me an important lesson: that internal resilience can be deliberately cultivated."[24]

> "[Eye movement desensitization and reprocessing therapy] taught me an important lesson: that internal resilience can be deliberately cultivated."[24]
>
> —Eva Holland, car crash survivor

Many other people have also found EMDR therapy effective. In a 2012 study published in the Journal of Behavior Therapy and Experimental Psychiatry, 77 percent of patients experienced decreased PTSD symptoms as a result of the therapy. The downside of EMDR therapy is that progress is gradual. People with PTSD often need many sessions to alleviate their symptoms. Also, mental health specialists suggest that the treatment might be overwhelming, particularly in the early sessions of therapy. The heightened fo-

MDMA for PTSD Treatment

When Lori Tipton was in her twenties, her brother fatally overdosed on drugs in her home. She subsequently cared for her mother, who suffered from mental illness. While under Tipton's care, her mother took her own life after killing two people. Tipton discovered the bodies of the murder-suicide. Soon after, Hurricane Katrina destroyed Tipton's home in New Orleans. The next year, she was raped. She experienced severe anxiety and panic attacks associated with PTSD from the multiple traumas. She tried standard therapy and medication, to no avail.

Tipton became interested in trying a new type of treatment involving the use of MDMA during psychotherapy. The experimental treatment is in clinical trials (in the United States, Canada, and Israel). As a patient undergoing this treatment, Tipton took a dose of pure MDMA and began speaking with two licensed psychotherapists while under its influence. MDMA is the active ingredient in dangerous street drugs (like ecstasy and molly), but some experts believe that in its pure form and combined with therapy, it can be useful in treating PTSD. Tipton explains that because of the treatment, she was able to mentally revisit her traumas without the usual feelings of terror and anxiety. She explains, "I was able to find such empathy for myself. I realized how much I was thinking this was my fault." A year after the treatment, Tipton is no longer experiencing PTSD symptoms.

Quoted in Will Stone, "MDMA, or Ecstasy, Shows Promise as a PTSD Treatment," *All Things Considered*, NPR, August 14, 2019. www.npr.org.

cus on the inciting trauma can be a trigger for patients with PTSD. A different treatment might be preferable for patients who experience extremely high stress levels following EMDR sessions.

Exposure-Based Psychotherapy

PTSD survivors engaging in avoidance behavior following their trauma often try exposure-based psychotherapy, also referred to as exposure therapy. This method asks people to physically or mentally revisit places or re-create scenarios related to their trauma with guidance from their therapist. The goal is to help people with PTSD overcome their trauma-induced anxiety so that they are able to confront the memories, see the people, and visit the places that remind them of their trauma.

Exposure-based psychotherapy can include any of four methods to help patients confront what they are avoiding. In vivo exposure is the direct confrontation of the avoidance. For example, if a person was robbed and physically assaulted in a park, the therapist would take that patient to the park where the assault occurred. Imaginal exposure encourages the PTSD survivor to imagine the avoided places or memories. Using interoceptive exposure, the therapist encourages the PTSD survivor to re-create the physical symptoms associated with fear and anxiety. To do this, the therapist has the patient hyperventilate to get an increased heart rate and shortness of breath so that these symptoms can be addressed. Finally, prolonged exposure is the combination of the three methods to work through trauma and symptoms. In a study published in 2020, mental health experts at the National Center for PTSD explain that prolonged exposure psychotherapy is highly effective in PTSD survivors and "has the strongest recommendation as a treatment for PTSD in every clinical practice guideline."[25]

Exposure-based psychotherapy generally includes eight to fifteen therapy sessions that last about ninety minutes each. This practice and CBT have been the most commonly used approaches to treat combat veterans with PTSD in the United States. However, Maria Steenkamp, clinical assistant professor of psychiatry at the NYU School of Medicine, questions the efficacy of both treatments. In February 2020 she told the *Military Times*, "We found that a third to half the patients respond well [to CBT or prolonged exposure therapy]. Of course that's the same way as saying two-thirds to half don't respond in a way that we would consider successful."[26]

Medication

Many PTSD survivors take medication in combination with attending psychotherapy sessions. Antidepressants known as selective serotonin reuptake inhibitors (SSRIs) are often prescribed to patients with PTSD. SSRIs raise the brain's level of serotonin, the chemical responsible for regulating mood, appetite, and sleep. SSRIs can take up to twelve weeks to become effective. When

Many people who suffer from PTSD benefit from a combination of medication and therapy. Antidepressants known as selective serotonin reuptake inhibitors (SSRIs) are often prescribed to patients with this disorder.

they do, the communication between nerve cells is improved, which helps a person with mood and anxiety issues related to stress. The side effects of SSRIs may include dry mouth, nausea, constipation, diarrhea, insomnia, and sexual dysfunction. When mixed with alcohol, increased drowsiness is likely.

Psychiatrists also sometimes prescribe alpha-1 blockers to help people suffering from PTSD with insomnia and nightmares. These medications work to decrease the brain's fear and startle response. Side effects of alpha-1 blockers may include low blood pressure, dizziness, and fainting. Medical experts say alcohol should be avoided while on these medications. Because of the potential side effects, a 2019 article from *JAMA Psychiatry* suggests that psychotherapy should be used before medication.

Psychiatrists report considering their patients' alcohol habits when they prescribe medication. According to the US Department of Veteran Affairs (VA), almost 75 percent of people who have experienced violent or abusive trauma report alcohol use disorders.

While Bobby Lane, a US Marine Corps infantryman, was deployed to Iraq, his unit was hit by five roadside bombs in an eleven-day period. Upon his return home, Lane suffered from PTSD. He experienced insomnia, had vivid nightmares, and tried to avoid traumatic memories by drinking alcohol. His symptoms were so severe that he contemplated suicide. Lane says that surfing brought peace and helped him manage his PTSD. In the documentary *Resurface*, about surf and ocean therapy, he says, "Now I see it, if life gets too hard, there's always the ocean."

Many other people suffering from PTSD also find peace in surfing. The Jimmy Miller Memorial Foundation and Operation Surf are nonprofit organizations dedicated to providing surf therapy to combat veterans who are coping with psychological trauma. Josh Izenberg, the director of *Resurface*, believes that surfing is effective in alleviating PTSD symptoms for many reasons. Among them, surfing requires singular focus, so it takes the person's mind off other stressful things or memories. Next, the waves of the ocean are cathartic and can metaphorically wash away negative emotions. Also, surfing is physically tiring and therefore helps encourage better sleep at night.

Quoted in Christopher Bergland, "Surf Therapy and Being in the Ocean Can Alleviate PTSD," *The Athlete's Way* (blog), *Psychology Today*, May 28, 2015. www.psychologytoday.com.

Alcoholism intensifies PTSD symptoms. Therefore, medical experts agree that alcohol use disorders must be treated in tandem with PTSD.

Alternative Treatments: Brain Training

Aside from medication and psychotherapy, there are less common, alternative methods to treat PTSD. For example, the process of neurofeedback, also called brain training, is in experimental phases, but it seems to be showing promise in treating PTSD. In a study detailed in the journal *NeuroImage: Clinical* in 2020, researchers concluded that brain training, the process by which participants do mental exercises to regulate their own brain activity, was effective in reducing PTSD symptoms. For about 61 percent of the patients in the clinical trial, symptoms were reduced so drastically that they no longer met the definition for PTSD. A person with PTSD has disrupted brain connectivity as a result of constantly being in fight-or-flight mode. Researchers believe that neurofeedback methods are successful because they help return the brain's connective pathways to normal levels.

The neurofeedback study involved twenty weekly brain-training sessions, during which researchers asked participants in the treatment group to reduce the activity of the brain's dominant wave, the alpha rhythm. Ruth Lanius, a researcher and psychiatrist, explains, "Participants were not instructed on how to reduce the alpha rhythm. Rather, each individual figured out their own way to do so. For example, individuals reported letting their mind wander, thinking about positive things or concentrating their attention."[27] When the clinical trial was complete, fMRI scans showed that the treatment group had increased brain connectivity.

Service Dogs and PTSD Symptoms

There are other alternative treatment options that seem promising but remain unproven clinically. For example, many people believe that service dogs are helpful in alleviating symptoms of PTSD.

Therapy like working with support animals is an essential part of any effort to recover from PTSD. It provides a way to understand and process the traumatic experience that is disrupting the person's life.

The VA, however, says that there is not enough evidence to support the claim. Therefore, while independent nonprofit organizations such as K9s for Warriors and Southeastern Guide Dogs are helping match veterans with service dogs, the VA is not providing veterans with that service yet.

According to these nonprofits, service dogs help soothe veterans with PTSD in a couple of ways. First, they provide companionship and distraction, which helps veterans cope with anxiety and panic attacks. The service dogs are also trained to stand directly in front of the combat veteran in a crowd to give the person extra space from other people. Regarding the effectiveness of service dogs for alleviating PTSD symptoms, Suzy Wilburn, who works for Southeastern Guide Dogs, told the *Military Times*, "The dogs are never going to be a cure for [PTSD], they're simply going to be a tool to help [veterans] in their recovery with it."[28]

Leaving Symptoms Untreated

When symptoms of PTSD go untreated, there are a variety of secondary effects. The person suffering from untreated PTSD often experiences some or all of the following symptoms: challenged interpersonal relationships, severe trust issues, chronic anxiety, isolation, low self-esteem, substance abuse, unemployment, self-harm, and suicidal thoughts or behaviors. Mental health experts agree that seeking treatment for PTSD is critical for the afflicted person's well-being, and early treatment in particular is most helpful. According to Dr. Adam Stern, an assistant professor of psychiatry at Harvard Medical School, individuals who have experienced a traumatic event should monitor themselves closely for symptoms and seek help early if any appear. Because the traumas that individuals experience are so different from one another, and brain chemistry varies so greatly from person to person, there is not a one-size-fits-all approach to treating PTSD. Some combination of psychotherapy, medication, and alternative treatments, however, might significantly alleviate PTSD symptoms.

Chapter Four

Living with PTSD

After the high school shooting in Parkland, Florida, on February 14, 2018, Kelly Plaur was plagued by nightmares and other PTSD symptoms. The gunman had fired shots into multiple classrooms, including Plaur's. Two students in her classroom were killed and four were injured. This was the source of her recurring night terrors. She is also triggered by window blinds, which remind her of the bullet holes left in the blinds of her classroom. She tells the *New York Times*, "Little things trigger me that I wouldn't think would trigger me."[29] About a year after the shooting, Plaur had to withdraw from a paramedic training program after experiencing heightened anxiety when she was transporting a gunshot victim. After withdrawing from the program, she told the *New York Times* that she was ready to try therapy.

PTSD After School Shootings

Sydney Aiello, who also survived the Parkland shooting, was subsequently diagnosed with PTSD. Two of her close friends had been killed in the attack. She graduated high school a few months after the tragedy and, according to her mother, suffered from survivor's guilt. College classrooms were a challenge because they were a trigger for Aiello. She tried to manage her symptoms with yoga, but it was not enough. On Sunday, March 17, 2019, just over a year following the Parkland shooting, Aiello took

Students grieve for the victims of the 2018 mass shooting at Marjory Stoneman Douglas High School in Parkland, Florida. Many survivors of mass shootings continue to struggle for months and even years after the event.

her own life. According to the medical examiner's office, she died from a bullet wound to the head.

Many survivors of mass shootings continue to struggle for months and even years afterward. A 2011 study published in the journal *Violence and Victims* found that 95 percent of survivors experience PTSD symptoms directly following a mass shooting, and a majority of them, 80 percent, continue to experience symptoms eight months following the trauma. Immediately following school shootings, communities come together in support of the survivors. Too often though, survivors continue to experience PTSD symptoms after the community focus has moved on. Time passes and life moves on for the community, but the survivors are still reliving the trauma. Rochelle Hanson, a psychologist specializing in trauma treatment, says, "What we worry about is people three or four months out who are still experiencing trauma-related symptoms. Those raise red flags."[30]

Many survivors of school shootings experience heightened anxiety in classrooms after the trauma. Meanwhile, some other triggers, such as Plaur's reaction to blinds, are less predictable. The common thread among PTSD survivors, though, is that the disorder can affect their everyday lives. Even after therapy, they might have feelings of powerlessness and avoid people, places, or things that remind them of their traumas. Sudden mood changes and feelings of isolation also might occur even after therapy. During times of heightened stress, PTSD from a previous trauma can further affect how the survivor eats, sleeps, and behaves.

Managing PTSD After Combat Experience

The type of trauma that causes PTSD is likely to affect the way that the survivor experiences its symptoms. Living with PTSD after combat is challenging because the veterans' military experiences often include both the best and worst times in their lives. Rachel Yehuda, a professor of psychiatry and neuroscience and director of traumatic-stress studies at the Icahn School of Medicine at Mount Sinai in New York, explains, "Treating combat veterans is different from treating rape victims, because rape victims don't have this idea that some aspects of their experience are worth retaining."[31] Combat veterans are often relatively young when they experience the horrors of war. But during the time that they are deployed, they also report feeling a sense of purpose and deep comradery.

When veterans return home, they face a different type of war. During their months of combat, they were surrounded by a natural support group. In their civilian lives, they find themselves alone or in the company of people who cannot relate to their traumatic experiences. They startle easily, sometimes causing them to react in ways they find embarrassing. Each night, many of them relive the horrors of battle in excruciatingly vivid nightmares. They struggle with the memories of what happened to them and what they did to survive. Some veterans experience symptoms immediately, while others have no symptoms at all until months after their return home.

Sebastian Junger experienced his first PTSD symptoms while he was waiting for a subway train a few months following his return from Afghanistan. While deployed, Junger was assigned to write a profile on Ahmad Shah Massoud, the leader of the Northern Alliance of Afghanistan. Junger and the people who accompanied him were forced to take cover while rockets rained down on their location for over an hour. He reports that the experience was traumatic and affected him for a few days after it had happened. Upon his return home, though, he did not consider it much, until the trauma overwhelmed him on the subway months later. He writes, "I found myself backed up against a metal support column, absolutely convinced I was going to die. There were too many people on the platform, the trains were coming into the station too fast, the lights were too bright, the world was too loud."[32] He sprinted out of the subway and went home. After that day, he had regular panic attacks when he was in crowded places. He was subsequently diagnosed with PTSD.

Working Through the Daily Struggle

Ryan Kaono was also diagnosed with PTSD following eleven deployments with the US Air Force. In 2005, during one of his tours in Iraq, Kaono's base came under attack. He tells the *Military Times*, "It wasn't my first mortar attack so I really didn't think anything of it."[33] He was securing classified documents in a safe when a mortar hit the building he was in. When the mortar shell exploded, he flew 15 to 20 feet (4.6 to 6.1 m) in the air before crashing down and hitting his head and right shoulder on a concrete barrier. He was treated at the hospital and notified that he had suffered a concussion.

When Kaono returned home, combat was never far from his mind. He suffered flashbacks, nightmares, anxiety attacks, and severe depression. Exhausted from chronic fear and uncertainty associated with his PTSD symptoms, Kaono swallowed an excessive amount of prescription drugs in hopes of ending his life. After he had taken the pills, he reached out for help. The Los Angeles

Suicide and PTSD

Matt McCarthy was a bomb technician for the US Army. He enlisted shortly after the terrorist attacks of 9/11 and served on many combat tours. After he got out of the military, McCarthy suffered from PTSD symptoms and attempted suicide. His wife, Heidi, persuaded him to seek help from a VA medical center in Georgia. To his family's surprise, the VA did not diagnose him with PTSD. Heidi and others close to Matt feel that was a mistake. He continued to struggle with his memories from combat. On July 30, 2020, he took his own life. Heidi says, "We were sitting outside together, enjoying the evening. I had come in for something. He came in the door, got my 9mm, and walked back out the door and I heard the shot." The VA reports that an average of twenty-two veterans a day take their own lives.

The National Center for PTSD explains that the risk of suicide is higher for people who have PTSD. The *Psychiatric Times* agrees that the associated symptoms of depression, anxiety, and survivor's guilt in veterans all contribute to the heightened risk for suicide.

Quoted in Josh Roe, "A Heartbreaking Story of a Veteran's Suicide and His Wife's Gratitude to the People Who Helped," News Channel 9 ABC, November 10, 2020. https://newschannel9.com.

VA hospital admitted him. After days of treatment and observation, he was diagnosed with PTSD. Regarding the management of the condition, Kaono says, "PTSD and living with it is a daily struggle. We're always cognizant of it. Those who are around us may see us and see absolutely nothing's wrong. We don't typically have external signs of our disability but emotionally and mentally, we still have to deal with it."[34]

There are many PTSD support groups for combat veterans to help them cope. While the VA offers standard treatment options, including psychotherapy and medication, there are also support groups for combat veterans that center on hobbies to help

> "PTSD and living with it is a daily struggle. . . . Those who are around us may see us and see absolutely nothing's wrong. We don't typically have external signs of our disability but emotionally and mentally, we still have to deal with it."[34]
>
> —Ryan Kaono, combat veteran

Black Horse Forge in Virginia (pictured) teaches blacksmithing to veterans who suffer from PTSD. In addition to learning a new skill, the participants develop a support system with others who share their experiences.

them manage their PTSD symptoms. The Combat Crawlers Veteran Offroad Association, for example, is a group for veterans to go off-roading in their vehicles. The group's mission statement explains that it is committed "to put[ting] an end to Veteran suicide through activities, activism and awareness."[35]

Similarly, in Fredericksburg, Virginia, there is a group for veterans to learn and do blacksmithing together to combat PTSD. In 2018 Steve Hotz and Dave Seitz, Gulf War (1990–1991) veterans, founded Black Horse Forge—an organization committed to teaching veterans a new skill while also giving them a sense of comradery. One of the participants, former marine Sean Mack, testifies to its efficacy. He says, "I hold everything in, and that might just be the Marine inside me, but I'm like a boulder. They've taught me how to take that boulder, crack it open and get some of that stress out and talk about it."[36] For combat veterans like Mack, a key component to managing PTSD includes finding a support group in the civilian world with people who understand the traumas they have been through.

Managing PTSD After Sexual Abuse

Support groups and loving partners are also critical for helping victims of abuse manage their PTSD symptoms. Melissa B. was sexually assaulted multiple times before receiving a complex PTSD diagnosis much later in her adult life. The first of many times that she was assaulted, she was four years old. The assailant was a neighborhood boy about seven years older than her. He made the molestation seem like a secretive game, which included her lying in the grass. She was so young that only years later did she recognize that what had happened to her constituted assault. As an adult, she loathes the feeling of grass. She also has flashbacks, nightmares, fear, and anxiety. During her worst moments, as her PTSD symptoms raged, Melissa began harming herself and developed anorexia.

Melissa knew she needed help. She reports that EMDR treatment and medical marijuana have helped her function for longer periods of the day and not have anxiety attacks. To further help manage her symptoms, Melissa teaches a comedy class. Comedy is her sanctuary. In an interview for Signed, X—a project created for sexual assault survivors to share their stories—Melissa says, "Performing has always been a place where that side of me is untouchable. I never have flashbacks while performing. I never have fear while perform-

> "I hate that I still feel like I have to have a reason to live, that I have to have a reason that I can even take up space in this world."[38]
>
> —Melissa B., sexual assault survivor

ing."[37] She also teaches improv comedy to trauma survivors and serves on an interpersonal violence task force at a hospital. Like many survivors of sexual assault who struggle to have self-worth, Melissa feels that she needs to prove her value. She says, "I hate that I still feel like I have to have a reason to live, that I have to have a reason that I can even take up space in this world."[38] She has also found that being in a personal relationship with a partner who understands her trauma and needs has been helpful as well.

Samuel Moore-Sobel acquired PTSD following an accident that caused an acute physical injury. His neighbors hired him for a day to help them move boxes. One of the boxes, containing items from a shed, exploded. He received second- and third-degree burns all over his face and arms from the sulfuric acid that had caused the explosion. Following the trauma, Moore-Sobel was plagued by frequent nightmares. He also relived the accident. The smells of rubber, the feeling of hot water, and the appearance of fire trigger him to reexperience the trauma.

Like many PTSD survivors, the disorder affected his self-esteem and was disruptive to his everyday life. After seeking therapy and taking medication, Moore-Sobel says that he monitors his diet and exercises regularly to help improve his self-esteem. For him, a supportive family has also been critical to move beyond his trauma. He further finds that nature soothes his symptoms of PTSD. He writes, "Over the years I have learned that healing is a choice, thrust upon us often at inopportune moments. It is choosing to be the hero in your own story by striving each day to become the person you envision yourself to be."

Samuel Moore-Sobel, "In Pursuit of Healing: My PTSD Story," Resources to Recover, November 7, 2017. www .rtor.org.

O (an alias to protect her identity) also reports that helping other women who are victims of sexual assault is personally therapeutic. O was born in Israel to parents with little education. Her mother was submissive and her father controlling. One night when she was in seventh grade, her father sexually assaulted her. O blamed herself and subsequently suffered PTSD symptoms, particularly anxiety and nightmares. She began psychoanalytic therapy as an adult. At age twenty-seven, around fifteen years after the assault, O confronted her father. He originally denied it before admitting it and blaming O's mother, suggesting that he molested O because her mother was a bad wife. O continues to manage her PTSD symptoms with meditation. In an interview for Signed, X, she says, "I've been doing meditation for about 10 years. . . . I learned to be very grateful for everything that is happening in my life. I recommend everybody meditate."[39]

Managing PTSD After Natural Disasters

Meditation and yoga after the earthquake in Christchurch, New Zealand, helps Bonnie Singh manage her PTSD symptoms. The earthquake, on February 22, 2011, changed her life. Singh was working in a tattoo shop as a receptionist and apprentice when the shaking began. As the brick building crumbled, a large fragment of debris hit her in the skull, breaking eight vertebrae in her spine—two in her neck and six in the middle of her back. Singh was able to dig herself out of the rubble, but her friend died from his injuries when the building collapsed. After the earthquake, Singh suffered from PTSD symptoms, especially survivor's guilt and depression.

Years later, she still experiences physical pain and emotional scars from her injuries. She tries to stay positive by immersing herself in her work as a tattoo artist in a shop she now owns. Aside from meditation and yoga to help her mental health, Singh also dances, sings, and writes down the things for which she is grateful each day. In an interview with the *Los Angeles Times*, she says, "Anything that uplifts you is the key. I'm not saying I don't get depressed—I do. It's something that comes with trauma. . . . It affects you for life. So I imagine I'm going to have to do this for the rest of my life. . . . But I know the tools. As long as I've got my tools, I'm OK."[40]

Lingering Signs of Devastation Trigger Traumatic Memories

The accounts of PTSD in the aftermath of Hurricane Katrina, one of the worst natural disasters in the history of the United States, are also substantial. A longitudinal study of 386 people from areas affected by the hurricane (conducted by researchers at the University of New Orleans, the University of Southern Mississippi, Stanford University, and Arizona State University) found that 50 percent of respondents experienced PTSD symptoms immediately following the natural disaster in 2005. Twelve years later, one in six respondents continued to experience PTSD symptoms.

Brandi Wagner was one of the many people whose lives were severely affected by Hurricane Katrina. Immediately following the storm's 125-mile-per-hour (201 kph) winds and devastation that killed eighteen hundred people, she left her battered home and lived in a camper outside of New Orleans for two months with her boyfriend's mother. Memories of the event stayed with her. When she returned to the city, the trauma hit her because the signs of the storm's impact were all around. In an interview with *Politico*, she says, "We could see the waterline on houses, and rooftop signs with 'please help us,' and that big X where dead bodies were found. I started sobbing and couldn't stop. I was crying all the time, just really losing it."[41] Wagner was one of many Katrina survivors who developed PTSD symptoms. She had anxiety, became depressed, and tried to avoid memories of the trauma with opioids and alcohol, eventually forming an addiction. She continues to take medication for depression, anxiety, bipolar disorder, and her opioid addiction—all problems that started with the hurricane.

Mental health experts suggest that to cope with residual symptoms of PTSD from a natural disaster, survivors should participate in trauma-focused psychotherapy if symptoms persist. Elyssa Barbash, a psychologist specializing in trauma and PTSD, further recommends deep breathing techniques for coping with anxiety associated with natural disasters.

> "Just because you have successfully completed treatment for PTSD does not mean that your work is over."[42]
>
> —Matthew Tull, University of Toledo psychology professor

Staying the Course

People with PTSD can recover and live normal lives, but mental health experts explain that they must be vigilant and persistent in caring for themselves. Matthew Tull, a psychology professor at the University of Toledo, argues, "Just because you have successfully completed treatment for PTSD does not mean that your work is over."[42]

Mindfulness and meditation are part of a regimen of self-care that can benefit people who have PTSD. These types of activities have been shown to alleviate some of the symptoms and enhance coping skills.

There are several ways that PTSD survivors can work to alleviate their symptoms. According to Recovery Village, which provides information and offers treatment services for substance abuse and co-occurring mental health disorders, there are many methods to cope with PTSD. PTSD survivors benefit from indulging in self-care, perhaps by getting massages or taking time to go for leisurely walks. They can alleviate symptoms with mindfulness or meditation exercises. Physical exercise is also beneficial to PTSD survivors, according to Recovery Village. Finally, mental health experts suggest that joining a support group, getting a therapy dog, and avoiding drugs and alcohol are all key to alleviating PTSD symptoms. The Centers for Disease Control and Prevention further recommends keeping to one's usual routine because habits are often comforting.

PTSD is a serious mental health disorder, but its symptoms are not insurmountable. Many PTSD survivors who have sought treatment and remain mindful of relapses and recurring symptoms have been successful in maintaining a normal life.

Source Notes

Introduction: The Challenges of PTSD

1. P.K. Philips, "My Story of Survival: Battling PTSD," Anxiety & Depression Association of America, November 19, 2009. https://adaa.org.
2. Quoted in James Risen, "Contractors Back from Iraq Suffer Trauma from Battle," *New York Times*, July 5, 2007. www.nytimes.com.
3. Philips, "My Story of Survival."

Chapter One: When the Brain Gets Stuck in Danger Mode

4. Eva Holland, "In a Crisis, We Can Learn from Trauma Therapy," *New York Times*, June 15, 2020. www.nytimes.com.
5. Quoted in Douglas Jones, "Fourth of July Fireworks Can Be Traumatic for Veterans with PTSD," WUSA9, July 2, 2020. www.wusa9.com.
6. Shaili Jain, "Avoidance: The Biggest Threat to Our PTSD Awareness," *The Aftermath of Trauma* (blog), *Psychology Today*, November 11, 2019. www.psychologytoday.com.
7. Matthew Tull, "Hypervigilance with PTSD and Other Anxiety Disorders," Verywell Mind, July 27, 2020. www.verywell mind.com.
8. Eristarisis, "A Balloon Popped and My Friend Had a PTSD Meltdown," In Real Life, October 7, 2020. https://inreallife .my.
9. Quoted in Sara Beth Guevara and Katie Hunger, "The Mental Health Struggle of Storm Survivors: It Follows Them Forever," Cronkite News, September 2, 2019. https:// cronkitenews.azpbs.org.
10. Quoted in Zahra Barnes, "What It's like to Live with PTSD After Escaping Domestic Violence," Self, April 19, 2018. www.self.com.
11. Erin Donovan, "My Mom's Violent Death Gave Me PTSD," Modern Loss, March 4, 2018. https://modernloss.com.
12. Donovan, "My Mom's Violent Death Gave Me PTSD."

13. R.E. Goldsmith et al., "Knowing and Not Knowing About Trauma: Implications for Therapy," *Psychotherapy: Theory, Research, Practice, Training* 41, no. 4, 2004, pp. 448–63.

Chapter Two: Scabs, Scars, and Reoccurring Injuries
14. American Psychiatric Association, "Patient Story: PTSD," 2021. www.psychiatry.org.
15. Quoted in Jeremy Hobson, "'I'm Still Dealing with It': How 2 Veterans Are Learning to Cope with PTSD," WBUR, August 7, 2019. www.wbur.org.
16. Quoted in Hobson, "'I'm Still Dealing with It.'"
17. Kenneth Vail, "Researching Coping Strategies for PTSD," *Atlanta (GA) Journal-Constitution*, June 23, 2018. www.ajc.com.
18. John Driscoll, "How PTSD Affected My Life," National Alliance on Mental Illness, February 19, 2020. www.nami.org.
19. Quoted in Stephanie Colombini, "For Veterans with PTSD, Life in Isolation Can Lead to Relapses and New Symptoms," KPBS, January 4, 2021. www.kpbs.org.
20. Quoted in NYU Langone Health/NYU School of Medicine, "Study Pinpoints Five Most Likely Causes of Post-Traumatic Stress in Police Officers," ScienceDaily, August 11, 2020. www.sciencedaily .com.

Chapter Three: Treatment Options
21. Concepción de León, "How to Rewire Your Traumatized Brain," *New York Times*, October 18, 2018. www.nytimes.com.
22. De León, "How to Rewire Your Traumatized Brain."
23. Bessel van der Kolk, *The Body Keeps the Score: Brain, Mind, and Body in the Healing of Trauma*. New York: Penguin, 2015, p. 3.
24. Holland, "In a Crisis, We Can Learn from Trauma Therapy."
25. Lauren B. McSweeney et al., "Prolonged Exposure for PTSD," National Center for PTSD, September 30, 2020. www.ptsd.va.gov.
26. Quoted in Patricia Kime, "VA, DoD Recommended PTSD Therapies Don't Help Many Military Patients, Review Finds," *Military Times*, February 4, 2020. www.militarytimes.com.
27. Quoted in Lawson Health Research Institute, "'Brain-Training' May Be an Effective Treatment for Post-Traumatic Stress Disorder, Clinical Trial Finds," January 25, 2021. www.lawsonresearch.ca.
28. Quoted in Diana Stancy Correll, "Is Adopting a Service Dog Right for You? What Veterans Diagnosed with PTSD Need to Know," *Military Times*, January 2, 2020. www.militarytimes.com.

Chapter Four: Living with PTSD

29. Quoted in Patricia Mazzei and Miriam Jordan, "'You Can't Put It Behind You': School Shootings Leave Long Trail of Trauma," *New York Times*, March 28, 2019. www.nytimes.com.
30. Quoted in Mazzei and Jordan, "'You Can't Put It Behind You.'"
31. Quoted in Sebastian Junger, "How PTSD Became a Problem Far Beyond the Battlefield," *Vanity Fair*, May 7, 2015. www.vanityfair.com.
32. Junger, "How PTSD Became a Problem Far Beyond the Battlefield."
33. Quoted in Deborah Aragon, "Living with Post-Traumatic Stress Disorder: A Veteran's Story," *Military Times*, 2021. www.military.com.
34. Quoted in Aragon, "Living with Post-Traumatic Stress Disorder."
35. Combat Crawlers Veteran Offroad Association, home page, 2021. www.combatcrawlers.com.
36. Quoted in *CBS This Morning*, "Gulf War Veterans Teach Blacksmith to Help Soldiers and First Responders," November 21, 2019. www.cbsnews.com.
37. Melissa B., interview, Signed, X, 2018. www.signedxproject.com.
38. Melissa B., interview.
39. O, interview, Signed, X, 2018. www.signedxproject.com.
40. Quoted in Rong-Gong Lin II, "When the Big One Hits, Emotional Scars Will Last for Years," *Los Angeles Times*, December 12, 2019. www.latimes.com.
41. Quoted in Christine Vestal, "'Katrina Brain': The Invisible Long-Term Toll of Megastorms," *Politico*, October 12, 2017. www.politico.com.
42. Matthew Tull, "Tips for Maintaining Recovery After Treatment for PTSD," Verywell Mind, June 24, 2019. www.verywellmind.com.

Getting Help and Information

Centers for Disease Control and Prevention (CDC)
www.cdc.gov

The CDC is the United States' public health agency. Its website includes information about the causes, symptoms, and treatments of PTSD. There are also psychiatry, psychology, and therapy locators to help people who are experiencing symptoms find treatment.

Mayo Clinic
www.mayoclinic.org

The Mayo Clinic is a nonprofit American medical center that treats PTSD patients, as well as engages in research regarding PTSD causes, symptoms, and treatments. The Mayo Clinic further publishes articles providing information to the public about a variety of PTSD topics, including how to help a loved one who is suffering from PTSD.

National Center for PTSD
www.ptsd.va.gov

Part of the US Department of Veterans Affairs, the National Center for PTSD conducts research and provides education on PTSD and traumatic stress. Its website presents useful information for understanding PTSD and offers the afflicted and their loved ones ways to acquire help.

National Institute of Mental Health
www.nimh.nih.gov

The National Institute of Mental Health is the leading federal agency in the United States for research on mental disorders. Its website provides brochures, fact sheets, and research publications on PTSD topics, such as symptoms, treatments, and coping strategies.

PTSD Foundation of America

www.ptsdusa.org

The PTSD Foundation of America is an organization that offers support services to combat veterans and their families. Its website offers basic information about PTSD, as well as links to a variety of news articles pertaining to veterans and PTSD.

Sidran Institute

www.sidran.org

The Sidran Institute is a nonprofit organization that helps people understand and recover from PTSD. Its website provides fact sheets and articles about PTSD symptoms and treatment. In addition, the website offers brochures and workbooks to high school students who have experienced and are trying to process trauma.

For Further Research

Books

Peggy Parks, *Childhood Trauma*. San Diego, CA: Reference-Point, 2020.

Bessel van der Kolk, *The Body Keeps the Score: Brain, Mind, and Body in the Healing of Trauma*. New York: Penguin, 2015.

Lindsay Wyskowski, *Living with PTSD*. San Diego, CA: ReferencePoint, 2018.

Internet Sources

Jessica Hamblen and Erin Barnett, "PTSD in Children and Adolescents," National Center for PTSD, September 16, 2019. www.ptsd.va.gov.

Jeremy Hobson, "'I'm Still Dealing with It': How 2 Veterans Are Learning to Cope with PTSD," WBUR, August 7, 2019. www.wbur.org.

Jan Hoffman, "PTSD and Burnout Threaten Medical Workers," *New York Times*, May 16, 2020. www.nytimes.com.

Eva Holland, "In a Crisis, We Can Learn from Trauma Therapy," *New York Times*, June 15, 2020. www.nytimes.com.

Shaili Jain, "Avoidance: The Biggest Threat to Our PTSD Awareness," *The Aftermath of Trauma* (blog), *Psychology Today*, November 11, 2019. www.psychologytoday.com.

National Institute of Mental Health, "Post-Traumatic Stress Disorder," 2020. www.nimh.nih.gov.

Jenny Taitz, "How to Reduce Your Risk of PTSD in a Post-COVID-19 World," *New York Times*, May 20, 2020. www.nytimes.com.

Matthew Tull, "Hypervigilance with PTSD and Other Anxiety Disorders," Verywell Mind, July 27, 2020. www.verywellmind.com.

Index

Picture Credits